Playing Synthesizers

A Beginner's Guide To Effective Technique

A volume in the Keyboard Magazine library for electronic musicians.

By **Helen Casabona** and **David Frederick**
Edited by **Brent Hurtig**

A **Keyboard Magazine** book

GPI Publications
Cupertino, California

Alfred Publishing Co., Inc.
16380 Roscoe Blvd., Van Nuys, CA 91410-0003

Art Director
Paul Haggard

Senior Editor
Brent Hurtig

General Manager
Judie Eremo

Graphic Assistant
Rick Eberly

Assistant
Marjean Wall

Director
Alan Rinzler

GPI Publications

President/Publisher
Jim Crockett

Director Of Finance
Don Menn

Editor: Keyboard Magazine
Dominic Milano

Corporate Art Director
Wales Christian Ledgerwood

Production
Cheryl Matthews (Director), Joyce Phillips (Assistant Director),
Andrew Gordon, Gail M. Hall, Joe Verri

Typesetting
Leslie K. Bartz (Director), Pat Gates, June Ramirez

Music Setting
Dale Herman, Elizabeth Arden Perry

Photo Credits
Cover: Paul Haggard
Page 5, 10, 36: Paul Haggard; 44: Ebet Roberts; all others are
courtesy of manufacturers.

Alfred Publishing Co., Inc. 16380 Roscoe Blvd.,
P.O. Box 10003, Van Nuys, CA 91410-0003.

ISBN: 0-88284-362-1

Item No.: 4110

Contents

Part I: Introduction   4

Getting To Know Your Instrument   6
Editing Controls; Performance Controls; Master Volume; MIDI Ports; Other Accessories.

Playing Around   9
Play Hard And Soft; Play Long And Short; Play High And Low; Try Moving The Wheels, Levers, Or Joysticks.

Part II: Using Presets   12

Lesson 1: **Brass And String Sounds**   13
Sounding Like Brass; Sounding Like Strings; Playing Idiomatically.

Lesson 2: **Keyboard Sounds**   18
Sounding Like Piano; Sounding Like Organ; Sounding Like Harpsichord; Sounding Like Calvinet; Playing Keyboards Idiomatically.

Lesson 3: **Bass And Lead Synth**   24
Sounding Like Bass; Playing Lead Synth; Playing Idiomatically.

Part III: Performance Controls   28

Lesson 4: **Pitch-Bending**   29
Pitch-Bending On The Synthesizer; Using The Pitch-Bend Device; Playing Idiomatically.

Lesson 5: **The Modulation Wheel**   37
What Is Modulation?; The Modulation Wheel; Playing Idiomatically; Modulation And Pitch-Bending.

Lesson 6: **Pedals And Preset Switches**   42
Pedals; Preset Switches.

About The Authors   47

PART I: Introduction

Now that synthesizers are becoming more commomplace than the home piano, many of us have had a chance to hear them first hand, and to play some of their incredible preset sounds. Some of those sounds are true special effects, such as ocean waves, spaceship landings, and dogs barking. Many of the most musically useful preset sounds, however, are imitative of other instruments—such as pianos, strings, lead guitars, and woodwinds, to name a few.

If you call up a bass guitar or trumpet preset on your synth and just play, you may get a sound reminiscent of a bass or trumpet—but your instrument will be falling short of its potential. In order to sound truly like a violin, for example, your synth has to be played like one, with the same musical expressions and idioms as a violinist would add to his or her instrument. After all, if you simply strummed a violin like a guitar, you might get some sound, but it wouldn't be the sound of a violinist.

Playing Synthesizers: A Beginner's Guide To Effective Technique, an excerpt from the book ***Beginning Synthesizer***, will teach you how to think idiomatically, so that your keyboard playing techniques match the instruments you wish to emulate. You'll also learn how to use your synth's pitch bend, modulation, and other performance controls—essential knowledge for making your music come alive. To benefit from the following exercises, all you need is the ability to read keyboard music, and the desire to get the most from your synthesizer.

If you wish to create your own sounds—as well as use your synth's presets—***"Programming Synthesizers: A Beginner's Guide To Editing Synthesizer Preset Sounds"*** is the companion Special Focus Guide to ***"Playing Synthesizers,"*** and will guide you step-by-step through the basics of synthesizer programming.

Getting To Know
Your Instrument

A violinist can pick up any violin and play it. It may have a slightly different sound and feel, and may even be a different size. But the basic concepts are the same: four strings tuned in fifths and a bow. From all outward appearances, synthesizers may not seem that similar to one another. Most have keyboards, but your instrument may have dials and your neighbor's may have buttons. Yours may have wheels and his may have joysticks. And if you're used to an analog synthesizer, the first bout with a digital instrument may be somewhat like learning to drive stick shift. But like the violinist, once you know one synthesizer, you should be able to apply that knowledge to playing others.

The first step to understanding your instrument is reading the manual, which we hope you've done thoroughly by this point. Then, whether you own a Casio CZ-101, a Roland Juno 106, or a Yamaha DX7, there are some controls common to all synthesizers that you should recognize. These include editing controls, performance controls, and a master volume (coded 1, 2, and 3, respectively in the accompanying three photos).

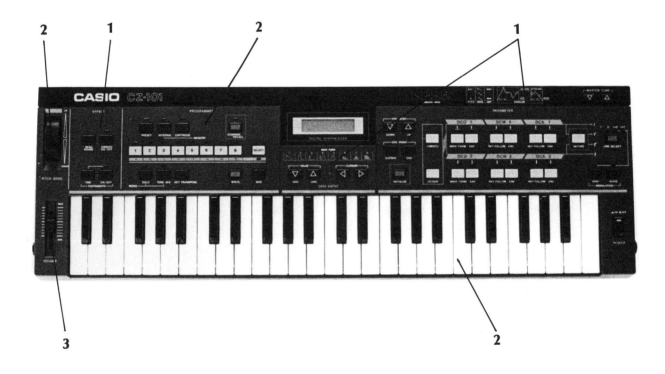

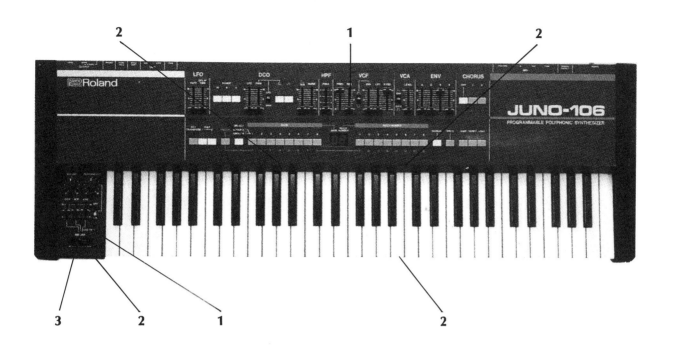

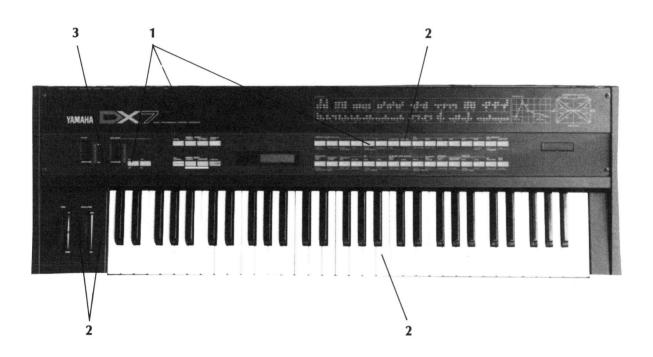

1 Editing Controls
2 Performance Controls
3 Master Volume

Editing Controls

Editing controls have labels like VCO or oscillator, Envelope Generator, LFO, and so on. They might be dials, buttons, membrane switches, or even sliders, but they all do the same thing: They allow you to create and tailor your own sounds.

Performance Controls

Performance controls are those you can play in live performance: Whatever you do will be played back immediately in real time. Performance controls your instrument is sure to have are Modulation and Pitch-Bend devices. These could be wheels, levers, ribbons, or joysticks. Your instrument probably also has controls for calling up presets (sounds already programmed and stored in your instrument's memory by the manufacturer). These controls are usually buttons or membrane switches.

Other performance controls are volume and sustain pedals, breath controllers, and the most important one of all—the keyboard.

Master Volume

All instruments have a master volume control, usually in the form of a dial or slider. This control allows adjusting the maximum level of audio output after the audio signal has been processed by all the other circuits in the instrument.

MIDI Ports

Most instruments these days have MIDI (Musical Instrument Digital Interface) capabilities. MIDI is an industry-wide specification that allows hooking your synthesizer up with other synthesizers, drum machines, and even personal computers, and controlling them all from one device (such as one of the synthesizers). If your instrument is designed to be MIDI compatible, the jacks for connecting the MIDI cable are usually on the back panel.

Other Accessories

Features your instrument may or may not have are a sequencer, arpeggiator, digital delay, memory-cartridge capability (for expanding memory space), jack for a breath controller, and even a video-monitor interface. We won't be discussing these features in this book; however, you should know if your instrument has them for use in the future.

Playing Around

If you haven't already, now's the time to start playing with your instrument to see what it can do. The best place to start is with your presets. Run through all your programs and see if you can pick out familiar sounds (piano, strings, horns, percussion) and be prepared for some very different ones. As you explore your presets, try these exercises to practice distinguishing between different sounds.

Play Hard And Soft

Assuming you have a *velocity sensitive* keyboard (meaning that it responds differently when you play hard or soft), see what presets sound different when you play hard than when you play soft. As you go, ask yourself these questions:

- Is the sound brighter when you play harder? Is it louder? Or does it sound less bright when you play harder?
- Does the sound change significantly when you play hard versus soft? Does the pitch change? Do you hear tones when you play it one way that you don't hear when you play the other?
- Does it make a sound when you play hard but remain silent when you play soft? Or vice versa?
- Is there no difference at all between playing hard and soft?
- Can you find a preset where you can get three or more different sounds, depending on how hard you strike the key?
- As you hold the key, try pressing harder. Does this change the sound?

Presets that emulate sounds of traditional instruments, such as strings, brass, and piano, and lead synthesizer presets are usually louder and brighter when you play them harder. Percussion sounds may actually change pitch depending on how hard you strike the key, and odd, alien sounds may change in even more ways. Some sounds, such as harpsichord, which isn't velocity sensitive in real life, may not change at all. And others may be pressure sensitive *after* you strike the key (this effect is called *aftertouch*).

Play Long And Short

Does it make a difference in tone if you hold the key down briefly as opposed to holding it down for several seconds, even if you apply the same pressure each time? Go through your presets again, and ask yourself these questions:

- Does the sound waver when you hold it long? Does the wavering repeat continually, or does it have a start and finish?
- Does the sound last for as long as you hold the key down? Does it last a fixed amount of time no matter how long you hold the key? Does holding the key down actually make it last less long?
- Does the note change in intensity over time? Get stronger? Weaker? Fluctuate? Does it change to a point and then remain constant until you lift up the key?
- Does the note actually change in pitch as you hold the key down? Can you find a preset where two pitches move in opposite directions?
- Can you find a preset where the sound doesn't begin until after you've held the key down for a second? Is there one where you

don't hear anything until you lift it up? Does it make a different sound when you lift up the key than when you depressed it?

Many percussion presets sound the same no matter how long you hold the key down; however, some may sound like a drum when you play it quickly, but sustain into a non-drum sound if you hold the key down.

Presets emulating traditionally expressive instruments, such as orchestral instruments, may have some natural vibrato (slight wavering in pitch) that you can hear when you hold the key down. Presets that make wind and ocean sounds may not even begin sounding until you've held the key for a second or two, and some presets, such as bomb sounds, may have four or five timbres that occur randomly over a period of several seconds.

Play High And Low

Some presets may sound different when you play on one half of the keyboard versus the other. This may be because your instrument has split-keyboard capability (you can program one sound for the lower half of the keyboard and another for the upper). It also may be that the preset is *scaled*, meaning the tone changes gradually as you play up and down the keyboard.

Try Moving The Wheels, Levers, Or Joysticks

Your instrument probably has two performance controls labeled Mod or Modulation, and Pitch or Pitch-Bend. These may be wheels, levers, joysticks, or ribbons. Try playing through your presets again, and this time, listen to what happens when you move these devices.

- What happens if you move the pitch-bend device? When does it seem musically useful to do so?
- What happens when you move the modulation device? Does it modulate the sound smoothly or do you hear a trill effect (jumping back and forth between two distinct pitches)? Try a string or brass preset. Now try a synth lead preset.
- Can you make a flat, uneventful preset change significantly by moving the modulation device?
- Find a preset with an obvious trill effect already programmed into it. Does the pitch change when you use the modulation device? If so, what part of the trill changes in pitch, the upper interval or the lower?

The pitch-bend device probably did something to all the presets, but it may be more useful with some sounds than with others. If a preset has many pitches already programmed into it, bending the pitch may sound like a mess.

The modulation device, on the other hand, probably affected some presets and not others. Presets for keyboard instruments, such as piano and harpsichord, probably aren't affected because those instruments don't produce modulation. Orchestral-instrument presets probably produce a smooth, continual pitch fluctuation when you move the modulation device, while some synth-lead and special effects presets might produce a trill.

PART II: Using Presets

What you hear when you first turn on a synthesizer may not be that musical. But your instrument can produce an incredible number of different sounds, ranging from strings, horns, and electric guitar to ocean waves, explosions, car crashes, and some you've never heard before.

Sooner or later, you'll want to learn to create these sounds yourself. But this takes time, and why shouldn't you get to hear what your instrument can do, now? For this reason, synthesizer manufacturers program their instruments with upwards of 50 to 100 different sounds, or *presets* that are stored in the instrument's memory.

What Are Presets?

A preset is a collection of control settings stored in memory that you can recall usually by entering a numerical code. These control settings indicate how the individual circuits (oscillators, amplifiers, filters, etc.) in the synthesizer interact with each other to create a particular sound. A collection of settings is also called a patch, from the days when synthesizers were *modular*, and each circuit had to be connected externally with patch cords.

Besides being a lot of fun, using presets is one of the best ways both to learn to play and to understand your new axe. The sounds a synthesizer makes are only the raw material of music. Once you have that material, you have to mold it to make it music. While this is true for any instrument, the way you play the synthesizer may vary, depending on the current patch. Just because you control pitch, dynamics (usually), and rhythm from a row of black and white keys doesn't mean you'll always want a traditional keyboard sound.

For example, call up a brass-like preset and play this:

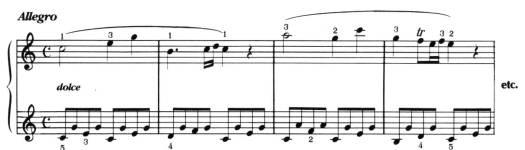

Sonata Facile by Wolfgang Amadeus Mozart.

Would a trumpet or French horn sound like that? Now call up a string sound and play it again. Would a violin or cello sound like that? Try it one more time, only use an acoustic-piano preset. How does it sound now?

Playing Idiomatically

The Mozart sonata above sounds best when played with a piano preset because the music is idiomatic for the piano. In music, an idiom is a sound characteristic dictated by an instrument's physical makeup. For example, a piano idiom is that you can't bend pitch; two violin idioms are that you can bend pitch but you can't play more than one or two notes at a time.

In the following three lessons, we'll show you that it takes a lot more than twiddling a few knobs and pressing some buttons to sound like the New York Philharmonic. That just as important as creating sounds is "playing" them. Whether your ultimate goal is to imitate other instruments or create entirely new sounds, learning to eclipse the traditional boundaries of playing a keyboard is half the battle to realizing the full flexibility of your instrument.

Lesson 1: Using Presets— Brass And String Sounds

What sounds come to mind when you think of a trumpet? How are they different from a string section of an orchestra? A trumpet player blows through a mouthpiece, and a violinist draws a bow across strings. Each of these actions causes air molecules to vibrate, which is the source of all sound. But the sound of air vibrations through a trumpet's cylindrical tube is a lot different than the sound of air vibrations in the wooden body of a violin.

Sounding Like Brass

Brass instruments include trumpets, French horns, trombones, and tubas. Although each of these instruments has its own unique sound, some idioms are common to them all:

- Notes that are "tongued" separately sound detached.
- Notes played quickly (such as trills) and pitch-bends are often (though not always) slurred. The trombone can also slide from pitch to pitch.
- You can play vibrato.
- A solo instrument can play only one note at a time.
- Brass sections tend to play together rhythmically (an effect you'd get on the keyboard by playing chords).
- Brass musicians often change pitch by changing the pressure in their diaphragm and lip, so large interval jumps are hard to make.

Call up a brass preset (find a bright one) and play this:

Paying close attention to the accent and slur marks now try this:

Both these examples are the same passage, but the first is notated with a keyboard inflection while the second has a brass inflection. What exactly is the difference? On a keyboard, such as the piano, you'd probably play the passage like this:

- You'd slur the quarter-notes, meaning that you would connect each note by not lifting your finger off each key until the next key is depressed.
- To get a clean trill, you'd play sharply, lifting each finger slightly off the key. Although the quickness of the notes makes them sound connected, a hammer hits a string each time you depress a key so each tone would have its own percussive thud, or attack.

On a brass instrument, however, you'd play the same passage something like this:

- You would "tongue" each quarter-note separately so they would be accented and not slurred.
- You would play the trill by quickly changing fingerings, not by tonguing each note (which would be difficult), so the trill would have a percussive attack on the first note, but not on the rest.

To play this passage with a brass inflection on your keyboard, hit each quarter note separately, putting a lot of weight into each key. To play the trill so it attacks only the first note, don't lift one finger off the key until you put the other one down.

Now let's look at some typical brass-section parts, and what types of brass presets work best with what types of music. Call up a French-horn sound—if your instrument has more than one brass preset, choose one that's less bright—and play this:

excerpt from *Water Music* by George Frideric Handel

What happens when you play the longer notes as opposed to the sixteenth-note couplets? Do the faster notes have the strength and substance of the others? If you compare a French horn sound to a trumpet, you'll notice that the strongest part of the sound doesn't occur at the beginning of the note, but some time afterwards. This is because when you blow into a French horn, your breath has to travel through several yards of tubing before it comes out as sound. To play French horn on the keyboard, you have to hold the key down long enough to emulate this effect, so French horn parts tend to have long, full chords instead of short or fast notes.

With bright brass, such as trumpet, however, quick, aggressive chords can be very effective. Call up a bright brass preset and try the passage below. Remember to hit the right-hand chords hard to get the spit of bright brass:

When you're playing a brass section you can play more than one note at a time, but you should always think in terms of how many horns are in your "section." In the example above, you might have four trumpets and a trombone: One trumpet is playing the top note of each chord, one the next note lower, and so on down to the trombone in the bass clef.

If you think of what most brass sections play, you can see how the two horn parts above are more typical of brass than, say, the Mozart piano sonata. There are a few reasons for this:

- Brass instruments have limited numbers of fingerings, so often, musicians change pitch by altering the pressure from their diaphragm and lip. This makes quick, large interval jumps hard enough that most horn players don't do them. Instead, horn solos tend to follow ascending and descending scales and arpeggios.

● Brass instruments can sustain and your brass sections should take advantage of this. For example, call up a bright brass preset and play this:

Sounds great, huh? Played with a piano preset, or any other sound with no sustain, the exciting effect is completely lost: Each chord dies out well before the next.

Sounding Like Strings

By strings, we mean those you play with a bow: violin, viola, cello, and double bass. (Other instruments with strings, like the guitar, mandolin, etc. are considered plucked stringed instruments.) To play a bowed stringed instrument idiomatically, you have to emulate the movement of the bow. There are several different inflections you can get with a bow:

● You can hold a continuous tone indefinitely.
● You can brush the bow across the strings to get a "detaché" effect, or bounce the bow to get staccato. (A note played detaché is cut slightly short and detached from the surrounding notes, but has a smooth, delicate sound; a staccato note is shorter still and sounds very harsh and abrupt.)
● Soloists play usually one note (and never more than two notes) at a time.

To play solo strings on the keyboard, you need a sensitive and expressive touch. Call up a string preset (a low string for cello sound) and play this:

Prelude from *Suite 1 for Violoncello* by Johann Sebastian Bach

Played as notated above—with no expression—this passage lacks sincerity as a string solo. When does the bow change directions? Where are the bow strokes strongest and weakest? Now try the same solo again, only play it as notated below, referring to these tips on string notation:

- The slurs indicate when you change bow directions.
- A ⊓ mark indicates a down bow (pulling the bow from left to right, and a V mark indicates an up bow pushing the bow from right to left).
- The long mark (—) over each G indicates that you should exaggerate the meter in this example (hold the note just a hair longer than a sixteenth-note beat).
- The o mark to the left of each G indicates an open string, which on a cello would ring into the following note.

Prelude from *Suite 1 for Violoncello* by Johann Sebastian Bach

To play this example with a string inflection, give more weight to the first note of each phrase, holding each "open" note while you play the next one. Make each phrase swell and then fade slightly at the end.

Another idiom of solo strings is how they play chords. Whereas on a keyboard you'd play something like this:

The fretboard of a bowed stringed instrument is curved, making it impossible to play more than two strings simultaneously. To play these chords on a violin, you'd have to roll the bow across the strings and play only two notes at a time, as notated below.

Solo strings usually play three- and four-note chords only in classical music. However, string sections are common in rock, pop, and most other contemporary music styles. In pop, you frequently hear violins singing in the background, holding long notes without too much movement. This is because stringed instruments are among the few instruments that can hold notes indefinitely. All you have to do is change directions of the bow to keep the note going forever. Strings use this prolonged sustain to create and release tension. For example, call up a string preset and play this:

The tension is created by the notes that hold over several bars, against the slowly descending melodic progression, because as listeners, we're not used to hearing notes last for so long.

Another effective string section idiom is "detaché," the effect strings get playing short, slightly accented bow strokes. Here's an example of what we mean:

Excerpt from *Barber Of Seville Overature* by Gioacchino Rossini

The detaché is in the left hand. To get the right inflection, place your fingers on the keys before pressing down, then play them not staccato, and not long, but somewhere in between. Try playing with varying pressures until you can hear the bows lightly brushing the strings.

Playing Idiomatically

Just as important as practicing inflections on the synthesizer is listening to the real thing. Put on some of your favorite music with brass and stringed instruments, and listen for idioms, both those we've discussed and any others you pick up on. Then practice the following two solos, first with a brass, and then with a string preset. Which is more idiomatic for strings? For brass?

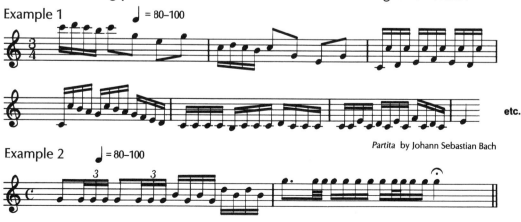

Example 1

Example 2

Partita by Johann Sebastian Bach

Lesson 2: Using Presets— Keyboard Sounds

This should be easy, you say, to play keyboard inflections on the synthesizer. After all, a synthesizer is a keyboard instrument, too. True enough—you'll get the best keyboard emulations on a keyboard synthesizer. But each traditional keyboard instrument has its own idioms, which in turn affect how you imitate them on your instrument.

In this lesson, we'll talk about the similarities and differences between a piano, organ, harpsichord, and clavinet, four of the most common keyboard instruments.

Sounding Like Piano

Let's start out with some piano idioms:

- No matter how legato you play, each note has its own percussive thud when the hammer hits the string.
- The notes have very little sustain—they'll die out seconds after being played no matter how long you hold down the key.
- The keys are arranged in *semi-tones* (pitch intervals of half-steps) and you can't play any pitches in between.
- The keys are velocity sensitive: The harder you play, the louder and brighter the sound.
- You can usually play as many simultaneous notes as you have fingers.

Because the piano is actually a percussion instrument, you can get a lot of sound from it. But since it has so little sustain, piano parts have to keep moving. That's why piano accompaniments in early rock and roll have a lot of motion. As an example, call up an acoustic piano preset and play this:

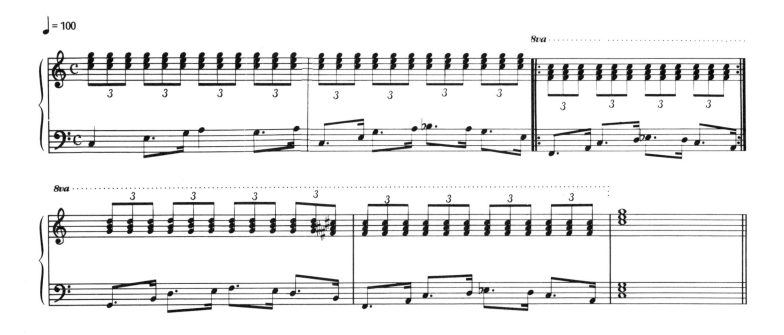

The same goes for pop:

Whereas a guitarist can bend strings to play between frets, or a violinist can slide along the fingerboard to get any pitch, on the piano you're limited to the 12 notes in the chromatic scale. To imitate pitch-bending and play "in the cracks," pianists play *grace* notes (notated as smaller notes). For example, here's how a piano would imitate a pedal steel in country and western:

By hitting one key and immediately sliding your finger onto the one a whole- or half-step higher (this works best going from a black key to a white one, or from white to white), you can get the impression of sliding up to a pitch.

Sounding Like Organ

The differences between the piano and organ are easy to recognize:

- Organs aren't velocity sensitive—you can't play loud and soft.
- Organ notes sustain for as long as you hold down the key.

Without dynamics, organists find other ways to get emphasis and play expressively. Call up a pipe organ preset and try this (play the fast notes by dragging the back of your finger across the keys):

If you were to try this same passage with an acoustic-piano preset, the climactic effect would be lost because it depends on sustain.

In addition to the pipe-organ sound (the kind of stuff mad scientists play in horror movies), there's the jazz organ, which has a percussive edge you don't get with pipes. Find an organ preset that sounds percussive and try the example below. The descending and ascending lines indicate palm glissandos: To play the descending glissando, key the chord and then drag the heel of your palm down the keyboard; to play the ascending glissando, do the reverse—drag the heel of your palm upward and then hit the chord.

Sounding Like Harpsichord

The harpsichord was one of the earliest keyboards and is therefore one of the more limited. It's not a percussion instrument, like the piano. Instead of hammers hitting strings, when you strike a key on the harpsichord a plectrum moves up and plucks the string, as you would pick a guitar string. As a result, the harpsichord isn't velocity sensitive and has very little sustain.

As with the piano, harpsichord parts should have a lot of motion. And since the harpsichord has even less sustain than the piano, you can play a lot of notes without sounding muddled. Call up a harpsichord preset and try this:

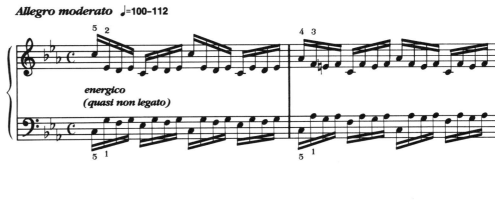

Praeludium 2 by Johann Sebastian Bach

However, you can't play sixteenth-notes forever. What if you want to play something like this, below?

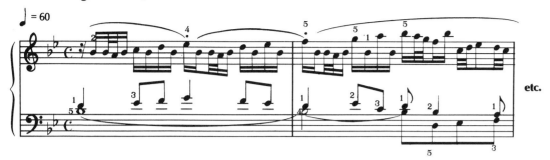

Partita 1 by Johann Sebastian Bach

No matter how expressively you play, there's not much you can do with this passage as written above. Now try this:

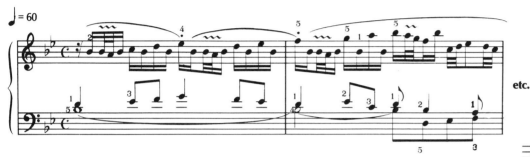

Baroque composers used a lot of ornamentation (like examples in Figures 1 and 2), to create emphasis, especially at the height of a line. When playing your own harpsichord parts, experiment with different types of ornamentation and other rhythmic variations to color musical events that on an organ would be sustained or on a piano would be played with dynamic expression.

Figure 1. Written-out notation for the first three ornaments in the Bach Partita.

Figure 2. Written-out notation for the fourth ornament in the Bach Partita.

Sounding Like Clavinet

The Clavinet is a clavichord with pickups. This gives it a real funky sound, popular in many contemporary music styles. When you strike a key on the clavichord, tangents (like picks) that are attached directly to the keys hit a string from below. The harder you play, the harder the tangent hits the string and the louder the note. (In fact, if you hit the key hard enough, you can even stretch the string to get a slight pitch-bend.)

Clavinet idioms are:

- velocity sensitivity
- no sustain
- sharp attack

A typical Clavinet part has a very sharp sound that's all attack. Although a Clavinet has no sustain, it can play dynamics. One of the most popular Clavinet idioms is therefore to play short notes very percussively—an effect you can demonstrate by playing one note repeatedly very fast and staccato by alternating hands.

If you really lay into the keyboard, the result is very exciting. To hear this idiom in a musical context, call up a Clavinet preset and play this:

Try it again with a harpsichord preset. Which one is more exciting?

Playing Keyboards Idiomatically

You can hear pianos, organs, and other keyboard instruments in almost any kind of music: classical, rock, rhythm and blues, techno-pop, and so on. Put on some of your favorite music and listen for how keyboards are used. Then try the four pieces of music below. Although any of them might work well with more than one preset, each one is idiomatic for each of the instruments discussed in this lesson: piano, organ, harpsichord, and Clavinet. Try them all. Can you tell which part is more idiomatic for which instrument?

Invention 15 by Johann Sebastian Bach

Example 3 ♩ = 60

Toccata and Fugue in D minor by Johann Sebastian Bach

Example 4 ♩ = 110

Lesson 3: Using Presets—Bass And Lead Synth

Synthesizer bass and lead styles are similar in that they're both derived from guitars: the bass guitar and the standard 6-string. However, whereas synthesizer "bass" parts stay pretty close to their bass guitar prototypes, lead synth has defined a style of its own.

In this lesson, we'll cover bass and lead synth, discussing both presets and tips for constructing your own bass and lead parts.

Sounding Like Bass

Providing the bass voice is perhaps one of the most useful things you can do with your synthesizer in any band or ensemble. You can free your bass player up to take on new musical functions, or if you don't have a bassist, you can fulfill the much needed role.

"Playing" bass (electric or acoustic) on the synthesizer is fairly straight-forward; however, there are a few idioms you should be aware of:

- You usually play only one note at a time.
- The bass part often supports the root of the chord. (To support a G chord, you'd play a G.)
- The bass usually provides rhythm.
- The timbre can vary depending on how the bassist plucks the string.

The standard way to play bass is by plucking the string overhand using your first two or three fingers. This makes a very even and consistent sound common to a lot of jazz and rock. For example, call up a bass preset—one with a fully round tone and not much twang. To get the best bass sound, experiment by playing hard and soft, long and short, and even legato and detaché to see if it makes a difference in the preset's sound. Once you've found a bass sound you like, try this:

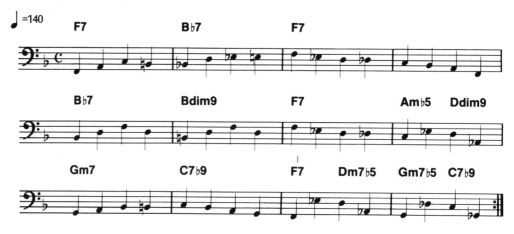

This bass part accomplishes the following:

- It provides a solid rhythm by playing on each beat of the measure.
- The first note of each measure is the root of the current chord.

In some music the bass may not lay the harmonic foundation for the tune or keep a rock steady beat, but it still provides rhythm. This is especially true in funk.

To play funk bass on the synthesizer, call up a bass preset that has a twang.

(Again, you may have to experiment by playing hard/soft, long/short, legato/detaché to get the twang.) Now try playing the example below, reading the notation like this:

- The accents (>) mark the beginnings of hammer-ons (when a bassist picks one note and frets the next without picking it).
- The accents (∧) mark where the bassist would pull up on the string to make it pop (the "doo-whop!" of funk bass). This is where you should make your "bass" pop, or twang.

Playing Lead Synth

The lead synth style found a place in rock and roll in the mid-'70s, and today has helped to define an offshoot of rock: techno-pop. However, the basic principle behind playing lead synth—improvising a monophonic line over rhythmic support from a band—was derived from the lead electric guitar and has been around for quite a while.

It takes years to learn how to improvise well on any instrument, and this goes for the synthesizer, too. (If you've improvised on any other instrument, you have a head start—you need only learn your keyboard scales.) Much of your technique you'll learn by practicing and *listening* to other soloists. However, here are some tips to get you started.

- Select a preset with a tone color that cuts above the other instruments you're playing with.
- Play your solo up high so it cuts above the rest of the band (think of Keith Emerson's solo from the '70s hit, "Lucky Man").
- Construct your solos around a recurring element, or *motif*.
- Give your solo a beginning, a climax, and an end.

Since the first synthesizers were monophonic, the one function they could serve was playing lead. Naturally, synthesists patterned their lead styles after the guitar, which had previously been the most common lead instrument in pop and rock. However, a keyboard is different from the fretboard of a guitar, and the two styles diverged accordingly.

For example, one way to create climax on a keyboard (which would be difficult on a guitar) is to build up a solo out of arpeggios (for those of you with eons of classical training, now's the time to pull out your arpeggios!). For example, call up a lead synth preset and practice this:

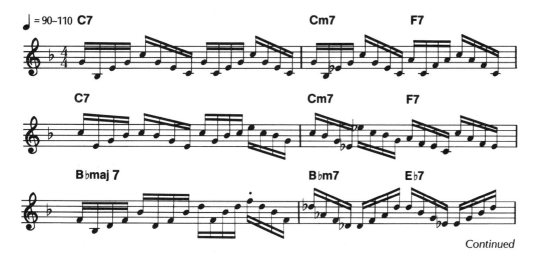

Continued

Notation continued from previous page.

Notice how the arpeggios create energy after you've built up to them with longer, more flowing lines that gradually get more complicated. After you've gotten this solo down, try each of these ideas to spice it up rhythmically:

- Accent the first note in each group of four sixteenth-notes.
- Leave a space before each note you want to accent (try this with a preset that isn't velocity sensitive to hear the full effect).

One way the above example creates climax is through the recurring arpeggio motif that gradually evolves throughout the solo. When you improvise a solo, you don't need to play something new each phrase; it's better to build a solo around a recurring motif. A motif can be a few notes or an entire phrase. You can vary motifs by playing higher or lower, changing the rhythm, inverting the melody, and adding filler notes.

For example, here's a basic motif followed by two examples of how you might build around the motif. After you play through our variations, fool around with it to come up with some of your own:

In addition to the elements of soloing we've discussed in this lesson, there's quite a bit you can do with pitch-bending and modulation, which we'll discuss in Lessons 4 and 5.

Playing Idiomatically

As always, the best way to learn any style is to listen and practice. Put on some of your favorite blues, rock, or jazz and try playing along. You can do this playing both lead and bass.

When you play bass, listen to what the bassist is doing to get some ideas. Start out by following the root of the chord, and then try to connect the roots with runs. Also, follow the rhythm of the song throwing in "pops" or "slaps," and "hammer-ons" when (and if) appropriate.

When you play lead, listen for any recurring motifs the soloists may be playing and try to build off them. Then try to come up with some motifs of your own.

On the following page is a bass part with an accompanying synth lead to get you started. If you can't find someone else to play with you, try recording the bass and playing the lead over it.

PART III:
Performance Controls

The first electronic instruments were by no means performance-oriented. Musical events had to be programmed at a much slower rate than they were actually to occur, and minutes or hours might elapse before you could hear the fruits of your efforts. Thirty years ago, a "live" concert featured a tape machine sitting onstage that played back the result of hours and hours of some electronic musician's work.

Today, luckily, we have voltage control and the microprocessor, so things work a lot more quickly inside your instrument. You can strike keys and hear the notes instantly. You can store sounds in your instrument's memory and call them up with the literal flick of a switch. The controls that let you do these things—your keyboard and preset switches—are called performance controls. That doesn't mean you can only use them onstage—just that you *can* use them onstage.

Performance controls include any control that can be played in *real time*, meaning that when you manipulate the control, you hear its effect immediately. The most common performance control is the keyboard; when you strike a key, you hear the resulting tone right away. In the following lessons, we'll discuss the most useful performance controls—other than the keyboard—that your instrument is likely to feature: pitch-bend and modulation mechanisms, pedals, and preset switches.

Lesson 4: Performance Controls— **Pitch-Bending**

The notes on a keyboard are arranged in half-step pitches that make up the 12-note chromatic, or equal-tempered scale. This scale is an artificial system consisting of equally spaced intervals that's been the basis for Western music for hundreds of years. (It's too lengthy a discussion to cover here, but if it weren't for this scale system, we wouldn't be able to play in more than one key on any given instrument.)

The human ear, however, can hear up to 25 different pitches in between each half-step. Most traditional instruments are equal tempered (the valves of a trumpet, frets of a guitar, etc.), but on many of them, you can play these "in between" pitches—or bend the pitch, so to speak—whether you use your breath, bend a string, or use a slide. In Western music, many of these pitch gradations—like rhythm and dynamics—act as inflections that not only color our music, but are natural elements of it.

To see what we mean, sing the "Star Spangled Banner." As you sing, listen to what happens to the pitch. You may notice that when you hit some notes (especially the "see" of "Oh say can you see"), you don't hit the pitch right on; instead, you hit a note somewhere below the pitch you want and then slide up to it. Instead of sounding atonal, this type of pitch bending colors the pitch you're bending up to.

Pitch-Bending On The Synthesizer

For all its fancy circuitry and sound capabilities, the synthesizer would be awfully limited if it couldn't bend pitch. That's why your instrument has a wheel, lever, joy stick, or ribbon somewhere to the left of the keyboard, labeled something like Pitch-Bend, or Pitch. In this book, we'll refer to a pitch-bend *wheel*, because this is the most common pitch-bend device. However, all pitch-bend devices do essentially the same thing: Move it one way and the pitch goes up; move it the other way and the pitch goes down. Try moving the device on your instrument to see which way is which.

The pitch-bend wheel is one of the most effective expressive outlets on the synthesizer, and good pitch-bend chops are as important as good keyboard chops. In general, rules for how to handle your particular wheel, ribbon, or whatever aren't carved in stone. But, here are some tips for finding what works best for you.

- Find a comfortable position for your left hand where you can move your fingers freely. Try using different fingers to move the wheel until you find a method that gives you the most control.
- Get a feel for how far you have to move your left hand from the keyboard to reach the wheel.
- Get a feel for how far you have to move the wheel to bend pitch up and down a half- and whole-step.
- The less pressure you put on the device, the better it will respond. Get a feel for applying the least pressure possible while retaining maximum control.

Using The Pitch-Bend Device

Let's look at all the different ways you can bend pitch:

- You can bend up (sharp) either off of a pitch or into a pitch.
- You can bend down (flat) either off of, or into a pitch.
- You can bend the beginning, middle, or end of a note.
- You can bend a note and either stay there or return to the original

pitch (unless the wheel is spring loaded, in which case it will automatically return to its center position).

- You can bend a note quickly or slowly.
- You can bend a small interval or a large one.

Here's a series of exercises to give you practice bending up and down over different intervals and taking different amounts of time to accomplish each bend. On this and all following musical examples, read the notation like this:

- A bend is indicated by a *glissando* line; you bend up if the line slopes up, and down if it slopes down.
- The duration of the bend is indicated by the note preceding the glissando line.
- A stemless note in parentheses indicates a duration shorter than a grace note.

In this first example, play the *G* on the keyboard and bend up to the *A*. The first notation in the example shows an almost instantaneous bend up from *G* to *A*, while the last notation shows a bend that takes two beats.

Example 1

This next example is similar to the first one, except you bend the middle of a tone (represented by tied notes): Hold the note for the duration of the first (tied) note, then bend up to the new pitch during the time value of the second (tied) note.

Example 2

Now try the same series of exercises, only bending down instead of up. (Play the *A* on the keyboard, hold for its alloted time and then bend the pitch down to a *G*.)

Example 3

So far, you've been bending off of one pitch up or down to another. Now let's go back through Examples 1, 2, and 3 and practice bending *into* a pitch. In Examples 1 and 2, instead of playing the *G* with your right hand and bending up to an *A* with your left, do this:

- Play a *G* with your right hand.
- Release the key just long enough to move your wheel down a whole-step without hearing the pitch go down.
- Play an *A* on the keyboard (if you moved the wheel accurately, you should hear a *G*).
- Move the wheel back to its center position (you'll hear the pitch bend up to an *A*).

On Example 3, do the same thing, only bend down into the pitch: Play an

A, release the key and move the pitch-bend wheel up a whole-step, play a G and then return the wheel to its center position. Keep practicing for both intonation and timing. After you get a feel for bending whole-steps, try the same exercises bending half-steps.

Another good pitch-bend exercise (that's a great lick for lead playing, too) is to play whole-steps with your right hand like this:

But bend the lower notes up a whole-step so you hear this:

This is the effect a guitarist gets by playing a note on one string and then bending a note up from a lower string to reach the same pitch. Try to make clean enough bends so you hear one note repeating but still get the guitar inflection.

The key to smooth and accurate pitch-bending is to make your hands work together as equal partners. If you're already used to playing keyboard, this probably means teaching your right hand *not* to play notes it's used to playing. At first, you may want to limit pitch bending to one-handed keyboard parts so you can keep your left hand on the wheel. However, sooner or later you should become familiar enough with your device to move quickly back and forth between it and the keyboard.

Playing Idiomatically

Now that you've developed some pitch-bending chops, try bending in a musical context. Here's a blues lick the way it would be played on the piano:

Now here's the same lick notated for synthesizer:

In the example above, you're faced with some choices on exactly how to bend the pitch: Should you bend off of notes or into them? Often, the choice is up to you. Play the lick again and try doing each bend both ways. Where does either method work? Where is one method preferable?

- To play the first bend in the passage, it's probably easiest to bend off the D♯ to the E.
- At the end of the second measure, you can't bend up to the B♭ as

notated by bending off the C. Instead you have to either move the wheel down and bend into the B♭, or play the A and bend up to the B♭.

A synthesist isn't limited to any particular pitch-bending technique or effect, but many traditional-instrument musicians are. What instruments can you think of that bend off of pitches and which ones bend, or slide into them? On what instruments can you bend up but not down? When can you bend both ways? Let's call up some presets to find out.

Bending "Brass" Like Brass. Brass players bend pitch using their lip in what's called a *lip slur*—any good classical or jazz solo is packed with them. A lip slur is usually a slight wavering of the pitch that's barely a half-step interval and sounds like a smooth, three-note trill. For example, call up a bright brass preset and try this:

Notice that on trumpet (and French horn, for that matter), you can bend pitches either up or down, returning to the original pitch right after the bend, and the duration of the bend is short. A trombonist, however, slides up and down over large intervals. Call up a brass preset (less bright than the trumpet sound), and try the trombone slides below.

Bending "Strings" Like Strings. Violinists and other string musicians bend pitch naturally when they slide their fingers along their instrument's neck. Although this slide is similar to a trombone slide in that it can cover large intervals and go up or down, a slide on a violin is usually more subtle. Especially in classical music, the musician's primary concern is to make a clean jump from one pitch to another (unless a glissando is notated).

Call up a low string sound and practice this next example. Try it first keying each note, and then again, playing the bend lines as described below (make sure your pitch-bending wheel is set for at least a major-third interval):

● In the first bar, play the F, bend up to the A, and bend back down to the F.
● In bar two, play the C♯ and bend up to the E, then quickly return the wheel to its center position right before you play the G. (Do the second set of bends in this measure just as you did in bar one.)
● In the third bar, play the E, bend up to the G, return the wheel to its center position right before playing the B♭, play the C♯, bend up to the high E, return the wheel to the center, and finish the measure.

To play this with a string inflection, move the wheel quickly to avoid overt glissandi but still get the sliding effect.

If you wanted to emphasize the glissando, you would move the wheel more slowly. This is an effect a lot of jazz bass players use. For instance, let's add some pitch-bends to the walking bass example from Lesson 3:

To play this with a bass inflection, bend off of each note preceding the bend line, and listen for the bassist's finger sliding up and down the neck of the instrument. This should give you some good practice bending pitch accurately over larger intervals, too!

Pitch-Bending And Lead Synth. When you're playing lead synth, you're not trying to imitate another instrument so you can bend pitches any way you want. However, as on lead guitar, bending up off of notes or sliding into them, is common. Here's how you might play the lead synth part from Lesson 3 with pitch bends:

As you practice this lead, listen to how the bends color the melody and create emphasis. Where do they occur? Knowing *when* to bend a pitch during a solo is as important as playing the bend itself. If you've played guitar or improvised on any other traditional instrument, you're probably already familiar with certain pitch-bend inflections—those that originated in blues. If you're not familiar with pitch-bending in improvisation, the blues, or pentatonic scale (so-called because it has five notes) is the best place to start:

- Position your right hand over a blues scale. In C, play the notes, C, Eb, F, G, and Bb.
- Without moving your right hand from that position, try bending in and out of each note, listening to which tones create melodic interest. Try bending up half-steps and whole-steps to give your phrase a major or minor sound.
- Practice this in all keys and see what effective bends you can find.

The best way to learn pitch-bending inflections is, of course, to listen to other guitarists and synth musicians. Listen for how pitch-bending colors both the phrasing and rhythm of their solos. Then try this synth rendition of "Good King Wenceslas" that features some of the pitch-bending techniques we've discussed so far. The lower two staves are a simple rendition of the melody, (either have a friend play that part with you or record it on a cassette) while the top staff uses pitch-bending to embellish the melody. Good luck!

Lesson 5: Performance Controls— The Modulation Wheel

So far we've discussed rhythm, dynamics, and pitch-bending as three ways musicians commonly color their music. Are there any other inflections you can think of? What happens when a violinist holds a high note at the climax of an expressive passage? What about when a sax player holds a note, alternating blowing hard and soft? In both cases, the musicians emphasize certain notes by making their tone waver.

- The violinist moves his or her hand towards and away from the bridge, making the pitch waver continually back and forth.
- When the sax player varies the strength of his or her breath, the volume of the note wavers between being louder and softer.

The wavering pitch and wavering volume are both types of *modulation*.

What Is Modulation?

To many musicians, "modulation" refers to changing keys in the middle of a piece. But in sound synthesis it means something completely different: Modulation is when some aspect of a sound—its pitch, volume, brightness, etc.—continually wavers back and forth. We've already looked at two types of modulation: the violinist's *vibrato* (a type of pitch modulation); and the saxophonist's tremolo (volume, or *amplitude* modulation). To understand what other types of modulation there are and how a synthesizer recreates them, we have to look a little at how the instrument works.

When you strike a key on the keyboard, a message is sent to the oscillator telling it to generate an audio signal. This signal is a *periodic* waveform, meaning that it repeats itself over time, or *oscillates* (see Figure 1). As the waveform oscillates, it produces a series of clicks. If the oscillations are very slow, all you hear are the clicks; as you speed them up, the clicks sooner or later blend together into what we perceive as a pitch (this first happens at about 20 oscillations-per-second). Because the speed of a signal determines its pitch, pitches are often called *frequencies*.

On a synthesizer, the audible signals are produced by a Voltage-Controlled Oscillator (VCO), and the sub-audio signals are produced by the Low-Frequency Oscillator (LFO). Modulation occurs when an LFO signal is applied to an audible frequency; while you can't hear the LFO signal, you can hear the effect it has on the higher frequency, or some aspect of that frequency. The type of modulation depends on what aspect of the sound wavers back and forth, and the shape of that wavering. On most instruments you can modulate pitch, loudness, and brightness:

- When an LFO signal is applied to the VCO, the pitch wavers above and below the note you originally played (*frequency modulation*).
- When the LFO signal is applied to the amplifier, the volume goes up and down (*amplitude modulation*).
- When the LFO signal is applied to the filter, you get spectrum (which has to do with brightness) modulation (a *wah-wah* effect).

The shape of modulation is determined by the shape of the LFO signal. To understand how different LFO waveshapes modulate sound in different ways, consider pitch modulation. Below are some of the most common LFO

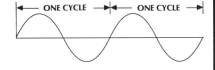

Figure 1. Two cycles of a sine wave: A cycle consists of one complete up and down repetition of the pattern.

waveshapes. In each of these graphs, the horizontal, X-axis shows what happens to the pitch over time; the vertical, Y-axis represents the degree of change in pitch.

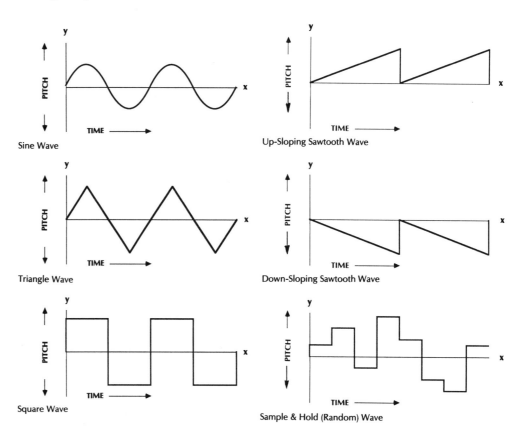

Sine Wave

Up-Sloping Sawtooth Wave

Triangle Wave

Down-Sloping Sawtooth Wave

Square Wave

Sample & Hold (Random) Wave

Look at each waveshape above and sing along with its shape, tracing how it travels over time from pitch to pitch. This is what you should discover:

- Sine and triangle waves produce smooth, continuous pitch fluctuations that cover all frequencies in between the two extremes. This is the natural *vibrato* sound you hear from strings, horns, and voice.
- An up-sloping sawtooth wave covers all intervening frequencies on the way up, but skips them on the way down (like a submarine emergency signal).
- A down-sloping sawtooth wave makes a clean jump on the way up but covers all frequencies on the way down (like a gun-shot sound that moves quickly to a climax and then fades away gradually).
- When you modulate a signal with a square wave, the pitch jumps back and forth between the two frequencies and no intervening frequencies are heard. This creates a trill. A variation on square-wave modulation is when the width of the modulating square wave modulates, or changes, too (see Figure 2). This is called *pulse-width modulation* , and creates a swirling effect that's like vibrato or tremolo but has a phase-shifter like quality.
- The sample-and-hold, or random modulation travels abruptly from pitch to pitch, randomly hitting intervening pitches along the way.

Now, go back through your presets and listen for these different waveshapes. What presets have vibrato? Trill? Sawtooth-wave modulation? How about sample and hold? In general:

- Orchestral and organ presets feature vibrato from sine- or

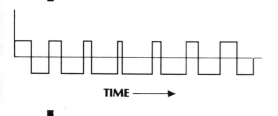

TIME ———▶

Figure 2. A square wave whose width, or duty cycle is being modulated.

triangle-wave modulation.
- Melodic synthesizer presets (e.g., lead synth, electric instrument sounds) sometimes feature trill from square-wave modulation.
- Listen for sawtooth-wave modulation in synthetic presets, such as sirens, ocean and wind sounds, and explosions.
- Listen for sample-and-hold modulation in computer- or robot-like sounds.

The Modulation Wheel

In presets that have modulation, the modulation either remains constant, or changes over time. In either case, however, whenever you play that preset, the modulation does the same thing. But what if you're playing a string solo on a patch that has constant modulation and you want to play some notes with vibrato and others without it? What if you want to introduce vibrato gradually, or fade it out?

To allow controlling and varying the *amount* of modulation as you play, your instrument has a performance control labeled Modulation or Mod. (Like the pitch-bending device, your modulation mechanism could be a joystick, lever, pressure pad, etc., however we'll refer to a Mod wheel.) Call up a preset and move your wheel back and forth. What happens? (If nothing happens, try another preset.)

The first thing you may notice is that, unlike the Pitch wheel, the Mod wheel doesn't have a center notch. Instead, it moves smoothly from a full off to a full on position. Also, you should notice that the further forward you move the wheel, the greater the intensity, or depth, of whatever modulation is going on. In general, the Mod wheel works like this:

- When you move it fully back (off), no modulation occurs, regardless of the preset.
- When you move it fully forward, the modulation reaches its maximum intensity as determined by the preset program.
- In most cases, the optimum modulation amount for a preset is somewhere in between these two extremes.

Playing Idiomatically

To get the hang of the Mod wheel, try it out with some familiar presets.

Orchestral Sounds. Almost all traditional acoustic instruments (horns, strings, woodwinds) and the human voice feature vibrato. Accordingly, presets that emulate these sounds probably have vibrato, too. With most presets, the modulation remains the same throughout the duration of the notes played. But vibrato idioms are more involved than that:

- You should introduce vibrato on long notes and rarely on short ones.
- You should start a tone with no vibrato and add it gradually, making it swell as the tone progresses.
- Vibrato on high notes tends to waver faster and between larger intervals than on low notes.

Take a look at this horn solo (the vibrato is indicated by the squiggly line above the staff):

To play this like a trumpet player, don't just crank the modulation wheel all at once. First, set the Mod wheel so there isn't too much vibrato to start with. When you get to the note you want to play, depress the key and *then* introduce vibrato gradually, letting it build to a climax and taper off.

Another effective use of vibrato is to color string pads. (A pad is played by a back-up section in an ensemble. It's usually played low in volume, and provides harmonic support for the melody.) Again, introduce the vibrato after you play the chord and let it swell gradually with feeling:

Lead Synth Sounds. Using the Mod wheel is as important in lead synth as pitch-bending. Although lead synth, electric piano, and other non-acoustic-instrument presets may have square-wave modulation (trill) instead of triangle-wave modulation (vibrato), you use the Mod wheel in much the same way.

Practice playing this fast run up the keyboard with no vibrato. Then introduce vibrato to a sustained high note at the peak of the phrase (remember, this vibrato should be fast and deep so move the wheel a little further forward than usual):

After you've gotten the feel for this, try some more complex ascending and descending phrases, introducing vibrato to all the important notes—notes that you'd emphasize on the piano by playing louder.

Modulation And Pitch-Bending

One reason why your pitch-bend and modulation devices are next to each other (and sometimes part of the same control) is so you can use them together. For example, you can get a very soulful, bluesy effect by introducing modulation at the end of a pitch bend:

To use the pitch-bend and modulation wheel together, you may have to modify your left-hand technique to make the transition from wheel to wheel as smoothly and quickly as possible. This will be essential when you want to introduce vibrato in the middle of a pitch-bend, and then continue with the phrase. For example, play the passage below, referring to the following guidelines:

- Bend the note up, making sure to hit the new pitch accurately.
- Quickly remove your hand from the pitch-bend wheel and place

it on the Mod wheel (if your pitch wheel is spring loaded, you'll have to keep a finger on it so it doesn't spring back to the center position).
● Introduce the modulation gradually, letting it swell.
● Fade out the modulation, return your hand to the pitch-bend wheel, and return it to its center position.

Sometimes, you may want to use modulation in *place* of pitch-bend. Go back to the music examples in Lesson 4 and try introducing modulation instead of pitch-bends where pitch-bends are notated. Don't worry if your pitch-bending and modulation sound awkward at first. As with anything, getting these chops down takes practice, patience, and listening to others.

Lesson 6: Performance Controls— Pedals And Preset Switches

There's a lot to do when playing the synthesizer: As if using two hands on the keyboard weren't enough, you also have your left hand jumping back and forth between the keyboard and Pitch-bend and Mod devices, and you're sure to want to change sounds in performance, both during and in between songs. How can you do this? Some performance controls that will help are pedals and preset switches.

Pedals are peripheral controllers that usually supplement features your instrument already has. For example, the keyboard may be touch sensitive, but a volume pedal gives you increased control over dynamics; your instrument probably has a portamento control and Modulation device, but if you can control these effects with your feet, you can do more with your hands. Presets, on the other hand, are controlled manually, but one quick motion instantly calls up a sound that you'd otherwise never be able to program during a performance.

In this lesson, we'll introduce you to some of the available performance pedals, and give some pointers on practical uses for preset switches.

Pedals

Two of the most useful pedal controllers are a volume (or voltage) pedal, and a sustain (or damper) pedal. You've probably realized by this point that no synthesizer has everything, but many have inputs for at least one of these pedals. Look on the back panel of your instrument. If you see any jacks labeled volume, voltage, damper, or sustain, keep on reading!

Pedals are not a new concept for keyboard players. If you've ever played the piano, you're familiar with a damper pedal, which increases the piano's sustain. If you've played organ, you're already familiar with a volume pedal, which is an organist's only vehicle for playing dynamically. As a synthesist, you'll become familiar with both.

Volume Pedal. A volume pedal works like the accelerator pedal in a car: The further down you press the accelerator pedal, the faster you go; the further you press the volume pedal, the louder the sound. (Volume pedals are also called *voltage* pedals, because what they actually do is control the amount of control voltage fed to the amplifier—the more voltage, the higher the volume.)

Now, if your keyboard is velocity sensitive, why confuse the issue by getting your feet into the act? With a velocity-sensitive keyboard, you can get dynamics by striking the keys with more or less force. However, once the keys are depressed, you no longer have control over the dynamics. (If your keyboard has after-touch—meaning that it's *pressure* sensitive—you can press down on the key *after* it's depressed to get an additional umph! out of it, but you still don't have absolute control over dynamics.)

With a volume pedal, however, you can depress a key, and *then* use the pedal to make the note swell, die out, swell again, and so on (depending on how much sustain the current patch has). Using a volume pedal is most effective with long, sustained passages where there's not much action going on on the keyboard. For example, call up a string preset and play this pad. Try to give it as much dynamics as you can just from the keyboard:

Not too much you could do with the dynamics, was there? Now try using a volume pedal and make the pad swell and fade.

A volume pedal doesn't work so well with presets that don't have much sustain, like piano, clavinet, and harpsichord sounds: It would be difficult, not to mention musically ineffective, to coordinate foot action precisely with quick finger action. Besides, there's probably enough motion on the keyboard that you don't need the pedal, anyway. But don't take it all from us. Try using a volume pedal on all your presets and see what effects and uses you can come up with.

Sustain Pedal. A sustain pedal is like the damper pedal on a piano (and the jack for it may even be labeled "damper" on your instrument's back panel). When you depress the pedal, any notes that you're currently holding down or that you play subsequently will sustain. The only real difference between sustain pedals and a piano's damper pedal is that most sustain pedals aren't sensitive to how far down you press them: They're either on or off.

Obviously, the sustain pedal is most effective with sounds that don't have much sustain (you wouldn't ever want to use this with an organ sound, though you should go ahead and try it once). The most common uses for the pedal are with piano, electric piano, and sometimes clavinet sounds. Call up one of those presets and play this:

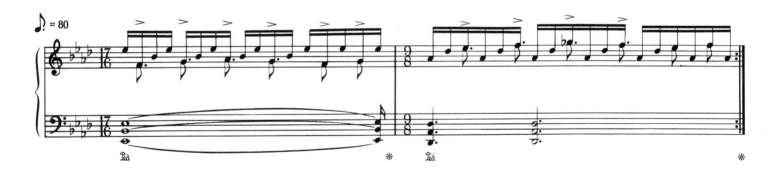

Normally, you wouldn't use a sustain pedal with string, woodwinds, and other horn sounds, but some parts may call for it. For example, if you're playing a passage with more parts than you can hold down on the keyboard simultaneously, you could use the sustain pedal to hold out tones after you release the key to move your hand to play another key. Call up a horn preset and try that technique on the passage below.

Other Pedals. In addition to volume and sustain pedals, there are a few other types of foot controllers you may be able to hook up to your instrument. Since most of these pedals are effects that are covered elsewhere in the book, we'll only list them here:

  • Portamento, or glide pedal. This pedal does no more than turn the portamento on and off.

- Modulation Pedal. This pedal works the same as a Mod wheel, lever, or whatever: The further you press it down, the greater the intensity of modulation.

Preset Switches

You've been using preset switches throughout this book and these are performance controls, too. In fact, they're among the most important performance controls because they allow you to radically change sounds in an instant. If you're playing alone in your studio, you don't have to program a sound every time you want to play it; if you're onstage, changing sounds at the flick of a switch is a must.

Calling up presets is fairly straightforward and there are only a few things to say about using them in performance:

- Don't change presets while you're holding down any keys: On most instruments, the sound won't continue smoothly into the next preset; it will either stop completely, or sound muddled.
- If you're a performer, you may want to organize your presets in the order you plan to use them over the course of your performance. If each preset has its own switch, you may want to organize them from left to right; if you call up presets by entering a number, you may want to put them in numerical order. In any case, make sure you're clear on where each preset is (this may sound obvious, but you'd be surprised at how easy it is to accidentally call up the wrong sound).

Perhaps the true art to "playing" your presets is coming up with creative ways of changing from sound to sound within a song. Here's an example using presets you're familiar with to get you started. Once you have a band, a buddy, or a tape recorder, your ideas should know no bounds.

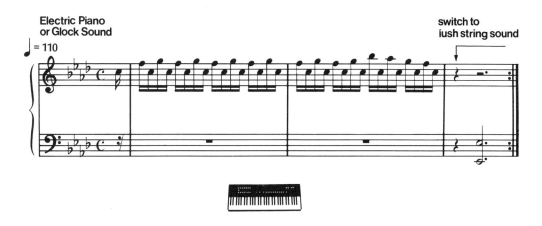

Jan Hammer

About The Authors

Helen Casabona

Helen Casabona grew up in the Washington, D.C. area where her musical education began at the age of six. She has studied piano, cello, guitar, mandolin, and several other stringed instruments. After graduating from Stanford University with degrees in English and Classics, she served as Assistant Editor at *Women's Sports & Fitness* magazine and also entered Silicon Valley's world of electronics by writing technical documentation for Hughes Aircraft, Intel, and numerous other firms. The co-author of *Beginning Synthesizer*, she also contributes to publications including *Frets*, the magazine for acoustic-string musicians, and *Cosmopolitan*.

David Frederick

David Frederick has been involved with electronic music since the age of seventeen when he studied synthesizers and electronic music production with Allen Strange. During his work in classical piano at San Jose State University, he continued his education in electronic and commercial music. After leaving college and earning his living through classical and jazz performances in the San Francisco Bay area, Dave accepted a position as Product Specialist with Passport Designs, a small music software company located in the coastal town of Half Moon Bay. While at Passport, he became an industry expert on MIDI, instrument interfacing, and computer-keyboard control. His knowledge of the wide range of electronic musical devices and the music manufacturing industry led to a position as Assistant Editor of *Keyboard Magazine*. While at *Keyboard*, Dave co-authored *Beginning Synthesizer*, and he is now a product specialist and technical writer for Waveframe Corporation in Boulder, Colorado.

Brent Hurtig: Editor

Brent Hurtig has been a consultant in music, recording, and broadcast technologies since 1977—both in North America and overseas. A musician and producer himself, he is currently senior editor for GPI Books, and is the editor of GPI's *Home Recording* newsletter. Brent is the author of *Multi-Track Recording For Musicians*.